—— ROBIN ELLIOTT

I0397141

TEAMS

A PRACTICAL GUIDE FOR DEVELOPING, MANAGING AND LEADING THE HIGH PERFORMING TEAM

BUSINESS
LEARNING
SOLUTIONS

—— QUICKBITES.CO

Copyright © 2017 Robin Elliott

All rights reserved. This book or any portion thereof may not be reproduced or used in any manner whatsoever without the express written permission of the publisher except for the use of brief quotations in a book review or scholarly journal.

First Printing: 2015

ISBN: 978-0-9925253-4-7

Quick Bites

32/101 Miller St

North Sydney NSW 2060

www.quickbites.co

QUICK BITES
BUSINESS LEARNING SOLUTIONS

TABLE OF CONTENTS

ABOUT ROBIN ELLIOTT i
PREFACE ii
COMPETENCY MAP iii
INTRODUCTION 1

PART 1 : UNDERSTANDING TEAMWORK AND GROUP DYNAMICS 3
WHAT AFFECTS GROUP DYNAMICS AND TEAM PERFORMANCE? 4
GETTING TO GREAT TEAM PERFORMANCE THROUGH THE SYSTEMS MODEL 5
QUICK BITES INSIGHTS 9

PART 2 : WHAT DOES A GOOD TEAM LOOK LIKE? 12
HIGH PERFORMANCE TEAM CHARACTERISTICS 13

PART 3 : UNDERSTANDING THE THEORY OF TEAMS 20
TEAM FORMATION AND DEVELOPMENT 21
WORKING WITH THE TEAM DEVELOPMENT MODEL 22
QUICK BITES INSIGHTS 30
TOP TEN TIPS 31

PART 4 : TEAMS ACROSS BORDERS 32
DEVELOPING THE HIGH PERFORMING TEAM WHEN IT IS GEOGRAPHICALLY DISPERSED 33

PART 5 : PERSONAL COMMITMENTS 36
ALIGNING OUR BEHAVIOUR 37
WRAP UP 38

PART 6 : TOOLS 39
TEMPLATES 40
CASE STUDY 42

FURTHER READING 48
WANT MORE INFORMATION? 49

ABOUT ROBIN ELLIOTT

Business and Leadership expert Robin Elliott is extensively qualified in people and operational management, having held C-Suite and Asia Pacific roles for a number of multinational and publicly listed corporations. Robin combines her rich corporate experience with a background in academic and executive education to bring you targeted and applicable developmental content.

Robin is qualified with a Bachelor of Business (Curtin University) and a Master of Management (University of Western Australia).

For a full profile on Robin see www.quickbites.co/author

PREFACE

QUICK BITES
Business Learning Solutions

Welcome to Quick Bites

Quick Bites is designed to provide 'bite-sized', digestible content for personal and professional development. Quick Bites products close the gap between current problems and desired outcomes by facilitating tangible skills development, ensuring personal and professional efficiency, effectiveness and productivity. Quick Bites will strengthen the key competencies required for self-leadership, and management of others, the customer and the business. Quick Bites books can be used as individual guides to help you build your commercial skills, ready-made workbook content for workshops and training sessions or supplementary material to focus and enhance your coaching activities.

At the heart of all Quick Bites resources is the belief that active self-enquiry and accountability is the way to build awareness and growth. The reflective and self-assessment exercises within Quick Bites are an important tool to engage you fully in the development process.

To help you synthesise the content and highlight the key practical points, Quick Bites presents you with a unique Insights summary at the end of each section. This feature helps you to quickly arrive at the main applications and understandings and accelerates your learning and skill development.

The practical application of useful theory, universal examples, exercises, templates and self-assessment activities will develop and strengthen the essential abilities required for personal and business achievement.

Use Quick Bites, and fast track your way to success.

COMPETENCY MAP

The content of this book and its learning objectives address the following competencies:

CLUSTER	COMPETENCY
MANAGING DIVERSE RELATIONSHIPS	• Understanding others
INSPIRING OTHERS	• Managing vision and purpose • Building effective teams • Motivating others
PERSONAL FLEXIBILITY	• Personal learning • Self development • Self knowledge
GETTING WORK DONE THROUGH OTHERS	• Developing direct reports

INTRODUCTION

"Great teams do not happen magically; they require conscious intent, deliberate action and constant maintenance"

While effective teamwork is essential in today's working world, the path to developing a high performing team is often problematic. Teamwork should be something that comes naturally, but with human nature as it is, working together successfully can be one of the most difficult states to achieve.

Teams are formed because they can achieve far more than their individual members can on their own, and while being part of a high-performing team can be highly rewarding, it can take patience and discipline to get to that stage. *Great teams do not happen magically; they require conscious intent, deliberate action and constant maintenance.*

An effective leader will create a work environment where people can achieve high performance not only as an individual, but as a member of a team.

The process to great teams is accelerated, and the difficulties minimised, when team leaders understand the key principles of group behaviour and the common stages that teams go through in their growth. Knowing what to do and how to lead your team as it moves through these stages of team development will be a crucial factor in your team's success.

REFLECTION

1. Think of a time when you have worked as part of a great team?
   What was happening, what were the key characteristics of this team?

   _____

   _____

2. Describe how you felt working in this team. Think about your relationships with fellow team members and the team leader.

   _____

   _____

3. What might be the potential barriers to team success?

   _____

   _____

PART 1

UNDERSTANDING TEAMWORK AND GROUP DYNAMICS

WHAT AFFECTS GROUP DYNAMICS AND TEAM PERFORMANCE?

Effective groups excel at teamwork because they have positive group dynamics. Group dynamics are the forces operating between people that affect task performance, relationships and team member satisfaction.

A team can be viewed as a system that converts inputs into three key outputs – task performance, employee engagement and customer satisfaction, as represented in Figure 1 below.

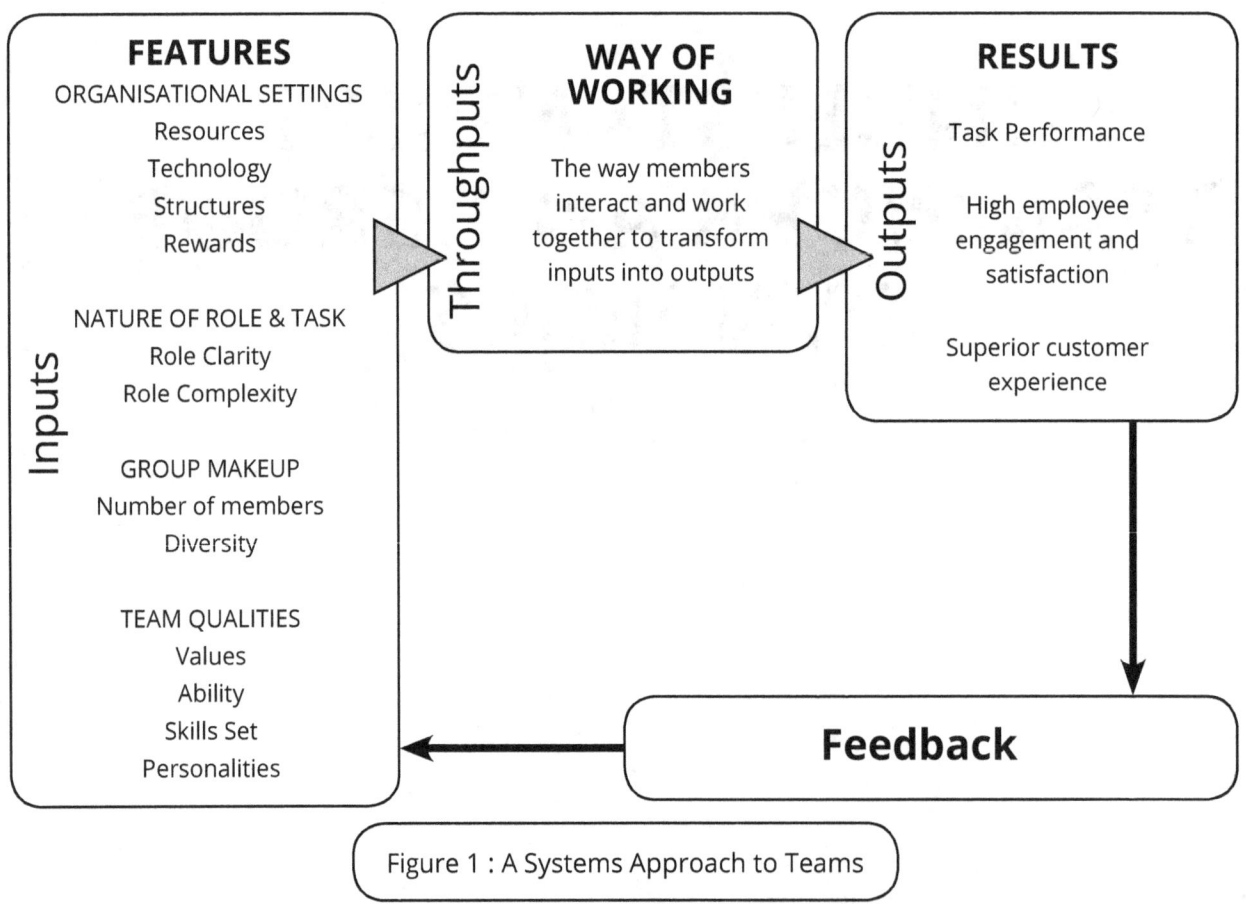

Figure 1 : A Systems Approach to Teams

PART 1: UNDERSTANDING TEAMWORK AND GROUP DYNAMICS

GETTING TO GREAT TEAM PERFORMANCE THROUGH THE SYSTEMS MODEL

"Have the right people in the right jobs in the right structure"

The systems model is a useful starting point to begin to understand and manage your team and improve its performance.

Team Inputs and Features: The Building Blocks to Great Performance

FEATURES

The organisational setting or context for the team is one of the major influences on team performance. Does the team have the right technology to enable it to get the work done? Are team members rewarded properly for their work? Is the team structured correctly to maximise the individuals' talents, skills and contributions?

Even though the inputs to a team's everyday work environment are sometimes out of a leader's control they are, never the less, factors that need to be addressed and redressed as required.

NATURE OF ROLE & TASK

One of the biggest factors for team disharmony and lack of performance is the unclear division of tasks and excessive or insufficient complexity of roles.

It is vital that each person knows what they are responsible for and that there is a fair and equitable spread of work across team members. When job responsibilities overlap, or accountabilities are shared, friction and conflict can occur as team members fight over their perceived job territory.

In addition, as people leave the team and new people join, role tasks and responsibilities can become further confused. Deliberate attention must be applied to the formulation of proper job descriptions and the clear delineation of roles.

TEAM MAKEUP

A high performing team is one that works with, rather than against, different thinking styles and skill sets. An effective team holds the view that difference strengthens rather than weakens a team, and that in difference, creativity and effectiveness are fuelled. Diversity can come from different genders, cultures and skill sets. Give consideration to the diversity in your team, and strive for it.

In addition, the size of the group impacts team performance. Teams can become unwieldy with too many members. A working group of between 4 and 8 people is usually an optimum size.

TEAM QUALITIES

Team qualities such as the values of the team along with the characteristics of the individuals in the team, their personalities and particular strengths, also impact team performance.

Deciding on a separate value set for the team, within the context of stated corporate values, helps to define the team's purpose and charter. Values help the team to establish common frameworks and expectations around behaviours. They establish what the team as a whole believe to be true. Values help to create an internal reference point from which decisions can be made and assessed.

Appraising individual's strengths and weaknesses, is akin to inventory management and is an important building block to assist you in the proper utilisation of team members. Right assessment means right people in the right jobs in the right structure.

PART 1 : UNDERSTANDING TEAMWORK AND GROUP DYNAMICS

TEAM WAY OF WORKING: THE KEY TO DIFFERENCE

Giving specific attention to *how* the team works together is the key to a team's and ultimately businesses competitive difference. A defined way of working ensures the optimum use of talents and skills and helps to manage conflict and difference.

Deciding on a way of working has several components and this topic will be explored in later chapters.

THE END GAME: TEAM RESULTS

"what counts is what gets measured and is what gets done"

Understanding what the team is meant to achieve, and being able to measure the team's performance, is the final step in the systems model. It is important to set defined team expectations and goals against a business time frame, and clearly communicate those expectations to the team. By-products of a high performance team are high employee engagement and superior customer experience, because what counts is what gets measured and is what gets done.

FEEDBACK

CLOSING THE LOOP

A high performing team is one that engages in constant communication and feedback. Constant assessment of team results against stated business goals is a necessary ingredient to ensure the team stays adaptable and current and is capable of performing the work.

Communication channels include regular team meetings, individual catch ups and performance reviews as well as more targeted team workshops to assess ways of working and team goals.

The systems model helps to dissect the many influences and inputs to great team performance. By ensuring all aspects of the team model are routinely addressed and monitored, the team will be set up for success rather than failure.

QUICK BITES INSIGHTS

A team is an interdependent system, with all parts needing attention.

Team outputs (results) depend on how well the inputs are converted.

The WOW of a team, its way of working, is how inputs are converted and is a team's transformational and competitive edge.

A key reason for team ineffectiveness is a lack of role clarity amongst team members. Know who does what.

Teams are dynamic. Ensure feedback is built into all aspects of the team's way of working.

What counts is what gets measured is what gets done, well.

ASSESSMENT

1. Using the systems model framework, what can you control as a LEADER in a team and what can't you control?

   _____

   _____

2. Using the systems model framework, what can you control as a MEMBER of a team and what can't you control?

   _____

   _____

3. Using the systems model framework as a guide, what are the key issues in your team right now?

   _____

   _____

4. Working within what you can control, and as either the Leader of the team or as a member of the team, what might be some first steps you could take to have your team work more effectively?

   _____

   _____

PART 1 : UNDERSTANDING TEAMWORK AND GROUP DYNAMICS

ACTIVITY: BUILDING THE TEAM FOUNDATIONS

Assemble the team and have some large flip chart paper on hand.

1. To help with role clarity, have each individual draw on the flip chart paper the main reason why their job exists (the purpose of the job). This should be a one paragraph, succinct statement.

2. Next, have each individual write down the key components of their job in broad terms. Think about accountabilities, how does the individual know when they have done a good job? What would they have accomplished?

3. Compare the charts of the team and look for obvious discrepancies, confusion and role overlaps.

4. As a team, agree on the roles of each team member and who does what.

5. As a team, agree on what good performance looks like. What results does the team need to achieve in order to succeed. Set performance expectations for the team that are measureable.

PART 2

WHAT DOES A GOOD TEAM LOOK LIKE?

PART 2 : WHAT DOES A GOOD TEAM LOOK LIKE?

HIGH PERFORMANCE TEAM CHARACTERISTICS

High performing team generally share common characteristics. These include:

- A clear and elevating team purpose
- Defined values
- Distributed leadership
- High trust
- Managed conflict
- Role clarity amongst team members
- Cooperative relationships
- Valued diversity
- Effective decision making
- Open and clear communication

Where to Start

Defining Purpose

Effective team leaders establish a sense of *shared purpose* by articulating a clear reason for why the team exists. They go back to the drawing board and state the fundamental reason for the team formation.

They then point the team towards an aspirational but realistic vision of the future. This vision serves as a goal that inspires hard work and the quest for performance excellence.

ACTIVITY

1. What is your team's purpose? Why does it exist? To help define your team's purpose, think about what would happen if your team wasn't there? What impact would the absence of your team have on the business unit or organisation?

   _____

   _____

2. What are you hoping to achieve in the next 12 months with your team? What vision are you working towards?

   _____

   _____

3. Paint a picture in words of how your team would look if it was a high performing team. What would be happening, how would team members be operating and behaving? What goals would you be kicking?

   _____

   _____

4. Translate this ideal picture, and the vision you have painted, into 3-5 goals for your team to be achieved in 3, 6, 9 and 12 months' time.

   _____

   _____

PART 2 : WHAT DOES A GOOD TEAM LOOK LIKE?

NOTES

Defining Values

Defining team values is an important step to ensure team success. Values are an internal reference point that serve as an anchor during times of change. They also help to provide an additional framework against which to make decisions and assess performance.

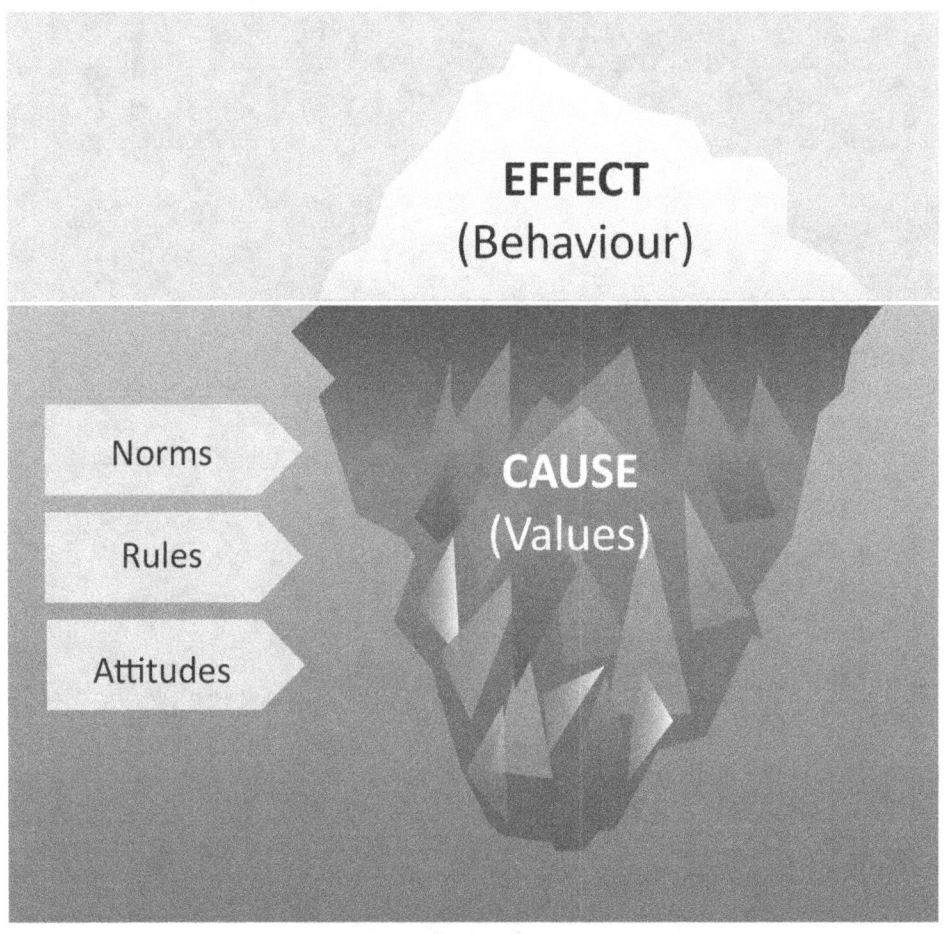

Figure 2:
The Iceberg Effect

As the diagram in figure 2 shows, values are the cause to the effect. Above the water line, 'visible' behaviour, is dictated by our beliefs and what we hold to be true. Values shape our attitudes, our norms and ultimately our actions. Attempting to change our behaviour without examining the internal, 'under the water line' beliefs that have driven that outward behaviour will only ever result in superficial change.

PART 2 : WHAT DOES A GOOD TEAM LOOK LIKE?

Stating Values

Values in a business context are typically stated as qualitative words. Examples of values are described below:

respect honesty courage
tact friendliness clarity innovative
moderation trust humility loyalty
discipline commitment team flexibility
collaboration responsibility
justice understanding diligence
assertiveness modesty confidence
unity creativity tolerance speed
patience
excellence

Assigning team values assists with defining a way of working and a team charter. Living the values, by using them to guide and assess results, ensures that they are meaningful and purposeful.

ACTIVITY

1. Decide on a maximum of 6 values for your team. If you have pre-existing and established corporate values, decide if there is one specific team value you can add.

2. As a team, outline what each value means to the team and how it looks in action. For example, a value of discipline may mean that the team always meets its deadline, a value of courage may mean that the team takes calculated risks. Come up with 4 or 5 statements (descriptors) about how the values look for your team.

3. Write each value separately on an index card. Write each statement (descriptor) separately on an index card.

4. Write the words "Aligned", "Somewhat Aligned" and "Not Aligned" separately on an index card.

5. (Card Sort 1) Ask the team, or subsets of the team, to place each value against the Aligned, Somewhat Aligned or Not Aligned Card. Once complete, review the cards and what has been placed next to them. What does this say about the values of the group, are the team in agreement? What needs to be done for the value that is either somewhat aligned or not aligned?

6. (Card Sort 2) Ask the team, or subsets of the team, to place the separate value statements (descriptors) against the Aligned, Somewhat Aligned or Not Aligned cards. Once complete, review the cards and what has been placed next to them. What do the results say about the specific areas to be worked on? Is there agreement amongst the group? Discuss and arrive at a resolution about how the team can best align their values and subsequent behaviours.

PART 2 : WHAT DOES A GOOD TEAM LOOK LIKE?

NOTES

PART 3

UNDERSTANDING THE THEORY OF TEAMS

PART 3 : UNDERSTANDING THE THEORY OF TEAMS

TEAM FORMATION AND DEVELOPMENT

Team formation takes time, and follows some easily recognisable stages, as the team journeys from being a group of strangers to becoming a united group with a common goal. These stages are universal, and will apply to both temporary working groups and a newly-formed, permanent team. As a leader of people, it is crucial that you understand these stages so that you may adapt your leadership style to suit and guide your team so that it becomes productive more quickly.

Tuckman's Stages Of Team Development Model

Psychologist Bruce Tuckman created the phrase "forming, storming, norming and performing" in 1965. He used it to describe the path to high-performance that most teams follow. Later, he added a fifth stage that he called "adjourning" to describe what occurs when teams change and disband. Figure 2 shows an overview of his model:

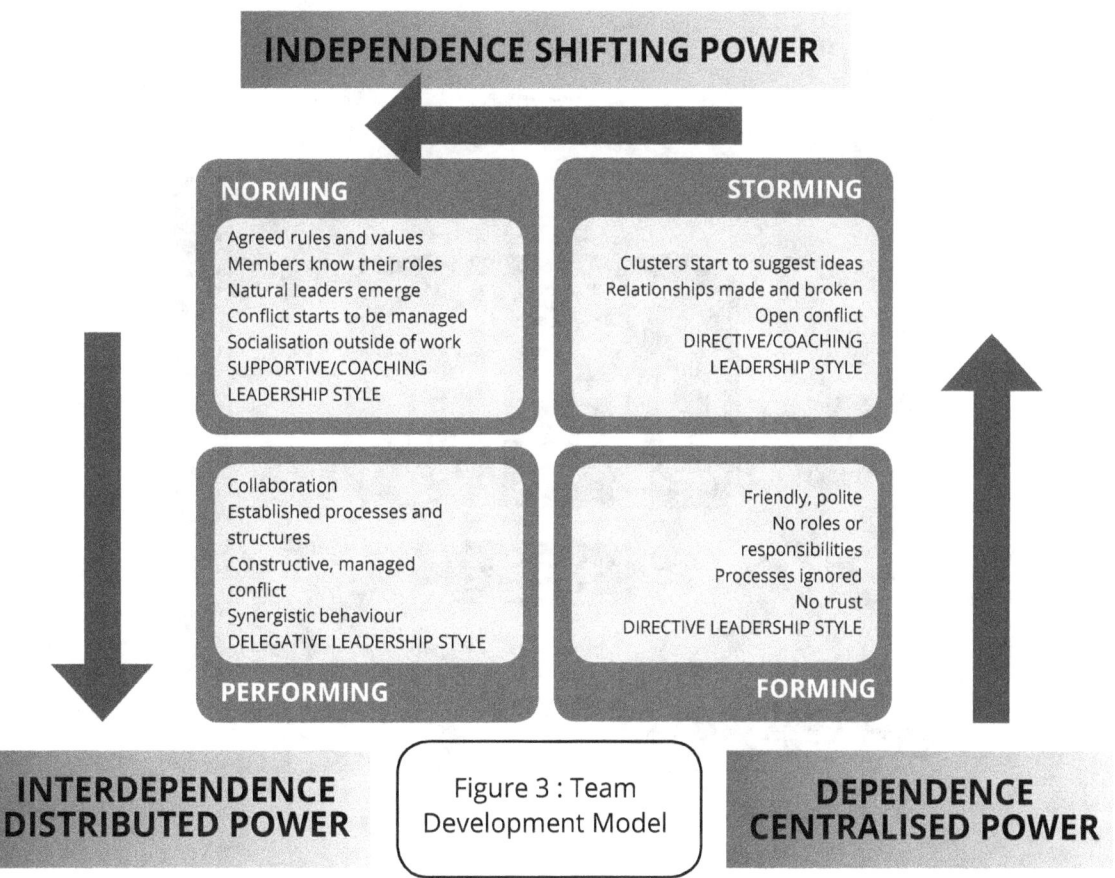

Figure 3 : Team Development Model

WORKING WITH THE TEAM DEVELOPMENT MODEL

The team development model is an insightful framework to help leaders navigate the often confusing behaviour that can occur amongst team members. It helps to develop and strengthen the essential leadership competency of managing people in groups.

Let's take a look at each of the development stages more closely and examine their applications in everyday work settings.

PART 3 : UNDERSTANDING THE THEORY OF TEAMS

FORMING
ORIENTATION AND PERSONAL TESTING

Teams start simply with people coming together and forming a group. This is the FORMING stage.

At this point, team members are polite, and are experiencing a myriad of emotions. The team is essentially a group of strangers with little interpersonal trust. Some members may be anxious, not yet knowing exactly what is expected of them. Others may be excited by the prospect of being part of the team. Typical concerns of members will be; *"what does the team offer me?" "what will I be asked to contribute?" "have I got the necessary skills to be an effective team member?"*

This may be a time when some members rely upon or become dependent upon another member who appears 'powerful' or especially knowledgeable. Such things as prior experience with team members in other settings can also affect how people come together.

This stage is typically fairly short, possibly lasting only as long as the first meeting.

Leader's Responsibilities at the Forming Stage

At this stage of the team's development the leader is responsible for bringing the group together and laying the initial foundations for team success.

Power and Leadership Style at the Forming Stage

At the forming stage, the power of the group is located with the leader. The leader naturally needs to be directive and controlling, given relationships are not yet formed amongst team members. Team members will be dependent upon the leader for direction and advice.

STORMING
CONFLICT OVER TASKS AND WAYS OF OPERATING

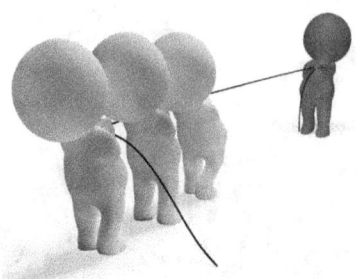

The storming stage is the time of team development when reality takes hold. Team members may jockey for position and seek clarification of their roles. The rules are beginning to be defined. Some people are ready to begin the tasks of the team, while others are not. The goals and worthiness of the team may be questioned.

This stage can be very emotional. Tensions emerge amongst team members, and there may even be outright hostility and infighting. Coalitions or cliques may appear around personalities or interests. Subgroups form around areas of agreement and disagreement. Individuals compete to impose their preferences on others and to become influential in the group's power structure.

Individuals may feel frustrated trying to accomplish goals and objectives for which they are held accountable when they feel that they have neither the support of established processes nor the support of fellow team members.

This is where conflict can derail a team and is the stage where many teams fail.

Leader's Responsibilities at the Storming Stage:

The storming stage is the period of time where the activities of the team leader are paramount. If a leader doesn't successfully steer their team through the storming stage, the team will fail. This is where the leader needs to be involved, hands on and strategic.

Power and Leadership Style at the Storming Stage

Team members at the storming stage are still dependent upon the leader to provide direction and advice, with the leader still responsible for assigning and allocating tasks. The leader should encourage information sharing, opinion giving and initiative amongst team members, as a way of encouraging trust amongst team members. This will facilitate the growing independence of the group and the distribution of power. The leader will use a directive/coaching style of leadership, with focus on task accomplishment and supportive relationships.

PART 3 : UNDERSTANDING THE THEORY OF TEAMS

NORMING
CONSOLIDATION AROUND TASK AND OPERATING AGENDAS

Cooperation is an important feature of teams in the norming stage. At this stage, team members begin to become coordinated as a working unit and tend to operate with shared rules of conduct. Most interpersonal conflict gives way to a precarious balancing of forces as norming builds initial integrations. Harmony is valued, but minority viewpoints may be discouraged.

Natural leaders emerge, and the team begins to work synergistically, relying on one another for advice and help. Individuals may start socialising together outside of work.

Individuals will start to identify with the group. Holding the team together and preventing its disintegration becomes an important objective.

Leader's Responsibilities at the Norming Stage:

In the norming stage the leader has the beginnings of a high performance team. There may be an overlap between the storming and norming stage, as new and more challenging tasks arise and the team reverts to storming characteristics. The leader needs to maintain vigilance and watch for any relapse. With time, and as trust builds among the team members, the norming stage will eventually stabilise.

Power and Leadership Style at the Norming Stage

The leader can loosen the reins a little and allow the group space to act independently. As trust increases amongst team members, the power of the group is shared and team members become less reliant on the leader. The team starts to be self-regulating and self-disciplined. The leader adopts a supportive Leadership style. The leader provides advice and guidance and focuses on building the relationships amongst team members through targeted team building events and the setting of guidelines for shared decision making.

PERFORMING
A STAGE OF TRUE TEAMWORK AND FOCUSED TASK ACHIEVEMENT

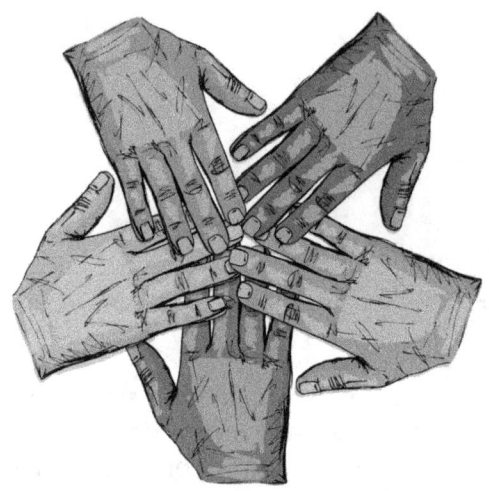

When the team reaches this stage, the members are working collaboratively toward achieving goals. The team is unified around a common purpose, shared values and identity. The processes and structure for accomplishing tasks are securely in place, there is role clarity in that each team member has clear knowledge about theirs and others responsibilities. There tends to be little, if any, destructive conflict, any conflict that occurs is quickly addressed and managed. The team is mature, organised and well functioning. It is a stage of total integration.

This is the stage where synergy and creativity occurs, where the sum is greater than the parts.

Power and Leadership Style at the Performing Stage

The team is operating as a well-oiled unit. It is self-regulating and self-disciplined. It is an interdependent team with distributed leadership. Trust amongst members is high. The leader adopts a participatory role in the team and a delegative style of leadership. Decision making largely sits within the group with little reliance on the leader.

PART 3 : UNDERSTANDING THE THEORY OF TEAMS

ADJOURNING
DISBANDING AND CLOSURE

Tuckman added a 5th stage to his model in recognition of the emotional reaction that can occur when a high performing team disbands. Teams disband either through organisational restructuring, or the finalisation of the project. As team leader, your concern is both for the team's purpose and goals and the team members. Breaking up a team can be stressful for all concerned and the adjourning or mourning stage is important in reaching both team goal and personal conclusions.

The break up of the team can be hard for members who like routine or who have developed close working relationships with other team members, particularly if their future roles or even jobs look uncertain.

TEAMS - A Practical Guide

SUMMARY OF LEADER ACTIVITY AT EACH STAGE

As a team leader, your primary goal is to help the team reach the Performing stage as soon as possible. Focus on developing the skills of:

1. DIAGNOSIS AND ASSESSMENT: the ability to assess the team's stage of development
2. INTENTIONALITY: being deliberate in choosing your leadership style, rather than going to "default-mode"
3. ADAPTABILITY: your ability to use a variety of leadership styles comfortably; and
4. PARTNERING FOR PERFORMANCE: the ability to reach agreement on what you and your team need from each other as you work together.

Stage	Leader Activity
Forming	• Facilitate team member introductions, e.g. formal orientation event, meetings, exchange of contact information and so on. • Outline the purpose of the team • Establish clear objectives and team accountability expectations, assigned tasks and roles • Provide resources for the team to do its work
Storming	• Assist the team in establishing processes and structure, identify an agreed way of working • Take deliberate action to resolve team conflict • Remind the team of why they have come together, what is the team purpose • Assist the team members in building good working relationships through targeted events and interventions • Provide support to individual team members who may be struggling • Remove roadblocks that prevent the team from accomplishing its goals • Provide timely feedback on the team's progress
Norming	• Allow the team to work more independently • Review the way of working and make adjustments when necessary • Provide support in the form of resources; training to develop skills and behaviours necessary to perform their jobs, and/or teambuilding events • Remove roadblocks that prevent the team from accomplishing its goals • Provide timely feedback on the team's progress
Performing	• Leader is overseeing a high performing team and is reaping the rewards of skilled leadership • Delegate as much as it is reasonable to do so • Allow the team as much autonomy as possible, trust them to work on their own with minimal check-ins • Acknowledge and celebrate the team success • Remove roadblocks that prevent the team from accomplishing its goals • Provide timely feedback on the team's progress
Adjourning	• Acknowledge the journey of the team • Highlight its successes and contributions • Allow team members the opportunity to voice their feelings about the disbanding of the team • Formally acknowledge the closure of the group. Encourage team members to move on. Paint a new vision of the future

PART 3 : UNDERSTANDING THE THEORY OF TEAMS

TEAM STAGE ASSESSMENT

1. Using the team development model as a guide, what stage do you think your team is in now? Explain why.

2. Is your team moving through the stages of development or is it stuck?

3. What insight/s has the model given you regarding the current state of your team and what you can do about it?

4. If you are the leader of the team, what leadership style do you need to adopt in order to progress your team to the next stage? What actions do you need to take as part of this style?

5. If you are a team member, what actions do you need to take to assist the team to progress to the next stage?

QUICK BITES INSIGHTS

All groups go through these stages of development and must spend time in each stage. If they try to skip a stage they will fall back into the forming or storming stage.

As a leader, you must steer your team through each stage.

Groups get stuck at the storming stage. This is where groups typically fail.

The stages are not strictly sequential, and very often oscillate between the storming and norming stages. Teams will also go back to forming stage when a new member joins the team.

Different leadership styles and activities are required at each stage. The leader must adapt.

Teams often fail because the leader can't let go of power. This will keep the team in the storming stage.

PART 3 : UNDERSTANDING THE THEORY OF TEAMS

TOP TEN TIPS

Teams don't just happen. They're built.
Use these tips to boost team performance.

1. **Agree on a Team Purpose**
   Establish the reason for the team's existence. Decide if the team wasn't there, what wouldn't get done.

2. **Develop A Unified Vision and Shared Identity**
   Have the team create their vision in order to build momentum and trust.

3. **Agree on a Rally Cry**
   Decide on a team rally cry or slogan. This should be aspirational and have meaning for the team. It can be an internal slogan that is used by group members only in order to remind them of the team's purpose. For example, "Go, Go" or "We Show The Way".

4. **Agree on Role of Leader**
   Paint a vision of what type of leader the team wants. Agree on the eventual role of the leader as being participatory, and agreement on what the leader needs to do in order to get there.

5. **Expose Irrational Rules**
   Once the team is established, check in and examine any rules or roadblocks that might be holding the team back, for example cumbersome administrative processes.

6. **Over Communicate**
   Be sure that people know what's going on organisation-wide, as well as all members knowing about team successes and failures. Knowledge and information should be shared at all levels.

7. **Establish Way of Working and Check In**
   Establish guiding principles for the team and an agreed way of working. Check in on this WOW framework at each stage of team development and adapt where necessary

8. **Build Team Spirit and Community**
   Hold short regular meetings, and ask each person to contribute. Encourage team members to get to know each other. Each team member should understand what the other has to offer in terms of knowledge, skills and abilities and how it connects to his or her own expertise and shared business objectives.

9. **Give Recognition**
   Give non-monetary rewards such as a thank you note, public praise, increased responsibility, special assignments, more autonomy, coveted work space etc.

10. **Celebrate Success**
    Share good news. Make noise about wins. Throw a party. Let everyone know when the team or a team member does something exceptional.

PART 4

TEAMS ACROSS BORDERS

PART 4 : TEAMS ACROSS BORDERS

DEVELOPING THE HIGH PERFORMING TEAM WHEN IT IS GEOGRAPHICALLY DISPERSED

Modern business frequently operates across large geographical areas. National, international and regional business structures build complexity into the dynamic of developing, managing and leading teams.

The principles of building a high performing team apply equally when managing across borders, with how team members communicate with each other becoming the major issue.

Communication and relationship building are obvious challenges with dispersed teams. Interaction between dispersed teams relies on technology that can be both facilitating and limiting. In these teams, technology becomes a critical component for effective and timely sharing of information. Because of the increased opportunities for miscommunication, it is critically important that the right technology for the team is utilised. In the case of dispersed teams that must rely on technology for communication; role clarity, defined purpose, vision and goal setting become critically important.

Dispersed teams have an especially challenging time in the Forming and Storming stages of team development since face-to-face interaction may be limited or even impossible.

TIPS FOR MANAGING THE VIRTUAL TEAM

Leaders can lessen the challenges for virtual teams by doing the following.

RIGHT TECHNOLOGY

Ensure that the technology chosen for communication meets the needs of the group and promotes ease of access to team members and other information. Look at all options, including social media to help team members stay connected.

COMMUNICATE

As with traditional teams yet even more so, clearly communicate the vision for accomplishing goals and objectives and clearly describe expectations for team member's results and behaviours.

TREAT TIME ZONES FAIRLY

With teams spread around the world, there is likely a short window when all team members are available. Rotate the times for meetings to make sure one member is not always waking up early for meetings and that another is not going home too late.

DISCIPLINED REPORTING

Use reporting to maintain communication and control. Be clear about instructions, and ensure that staff are accountable. Set tasks that focus on a specific outcome, and be clear about when you want the tasks finished. Introduce a weekly report for your team members to complete, confirming the work they've done. Disciplined reporting ensures the team leader stays on top of team activity, as well as keeping all team members accountable.

DISCIPLINED CONNECTING

Being a virtual team does not mean that individuals work in isolation. Team members need to be in regular contact with each other both in 'one on one' situations and team meetings. Utilise the technology available for staying in touch and implement regular virtual formal meetings in addition to encouraging informal virtual meetings.

UTILISE TOOLS

Utilise tools such as Skype to maintain visual contact during calls. Consider chat rooms, social media and on line meeting facilities to emulate as much as possible face to face contact.

COMMIT TO FACE-TO-FACE CONTACT

Nothing replaces face to face, personal contact. Make a commitment to meet physically in a central location, as often as is reasonably possible for social and business interaction.

PART 4 : TEAMS ACROSS BORDERS

VIRTUAL TEAM ASSESSMENT

1. What's working well with our virtual team right now?

   _____
   _____

2. What's not working well?

   _____
   _____

3. What can be done to improve the virtual team performance?

   _____
   _____

4. What steps need to be taken to ensure that these ideas are actioned? Develop an action plan and assign accountabilities.

   _____
   _____

PART 5

PERSONAL COMMITMENTS

PART 5 : PERSONAL COMMITMENTS

ALIGNING OUR BEHAVIOUR

Change happens when we are able to align our actions with new knowledge. When we make internal commitments to change and do better.

To ensure you develop and build your skills in managing teams, decide on some personal commitments now. What are you going to stop/start/continue in order to ensure your behaviour is aligned to your new level of knowledge?

Start	STOP	Continue

TEAMS - A Practical Guide

WRAP UP

What have been your key insights from this Quick Bites book?

_____
_____
_____
_____
_____
_____
_____

What is the one thing you can do today to activate your learning?

_____
_____
_____
_____
_____
_____
_____

"Things do not change; we change."
-Henry David Thoreau

PART 6

TOOLS

TEMPLATES AND CASE STUDY

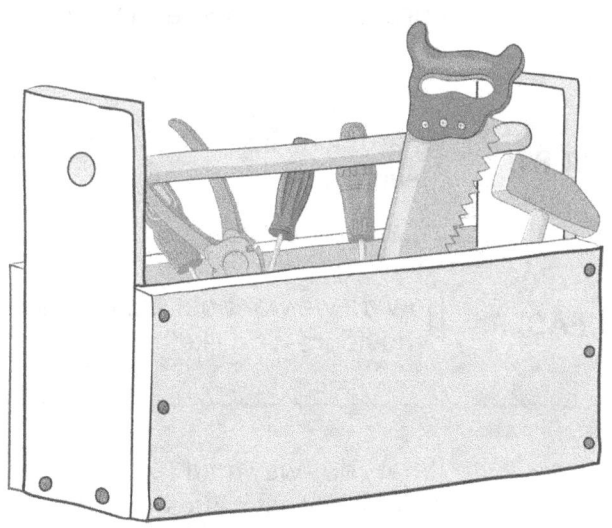

TEMPLATES

Template 1

Getting To High Performance: First Steps

Activity: As a team or in assigned groups, decide the following:

Key Activity	Questions
TEAM PURPOSE	Why do we exist as a team? What would not get done if the team did not exist?
TEAM VISION	What would the team look like when it has realised its purpose and is operating at high performance?
BRAND OR RALLY CRY	What is our internal slogan that is fun, aspirational and meaningful?
AGREED ROLE OF LEADER	How do we want our Leader to lead us? What are the key behaviours we'd like to see?
TEAM VALUES	What do we hold to be true? How will we model organisational values? Is there a specific team value we'd like to adopt?
WAY OF WORKING	What are our guiding principles? What will and won't we tolerate from each other?

PART 6 : TOOLS

Template 2

Team Stage Check In

Date: _____

Stage Of Team Development	What's Happening	What Do I (Leader) Need To Do?	What Does The Team Need To Do?
STORMING			
FORMING			
NORMING			
PERFORMING			

CASE STUDY

Case studies allow you to apply the knowledge and quick bites insights to a practical situation. A case study brings the theory and content 'to life' by describing a recognisable scenario which you can then analyse by using the new knowledge you have obtained.

Your analysis will help you to achieve greater understanding of the theory and concepts. It will also help to anchor your learning and develop new behaviours.

This case study can be completed as a self-study exercise, although it is best done in groups of 2-4. Read the case study alone and then as a group discuss your answers.

PART 6 : TOOLS

CASE STUDY

EMILY JOINS THE TEAM

Emily has been working with your company for 3 years. She is seen as high potential talent and a great worker with a strong team and work ethic.

Because of Emily's great performance she has just been promoted into your team. As the Manager of the team, you're excited to have her on board as you are sure she'll add value.

You think the team is working pretty well, although it could be better. You do have issues with quality control, and there has been some recent conflict between 4 of the team members. Given there's only 6 people in the team, this conflict has seemed to have repercussions. It appears that people may even be taking sides, and last month one person resigned, which is why you've been able to recruit Emily to fill the vacancy.

You've left the conflict alone for now, assuming that Emily joining the team will give everyone a fresh start, and that the team members will naturally work out their differences.

Most of the existing team members know Emily, given she's been working in an associated business unit. You assume she'll need minimal introductions. You've spoken to the team about her joining and suggested to the team that they all go out for lunch as a welcoming gesture.

You did hold a half day workshop 6 months ago, related to some new technology that had been introduced to the business. You combined this skills building session with some discussion around how the team could work better. Some of the team members openly challenged your management style, and were negative. Because of this, you thought it best to shut the discussion down. You haven't repeated the exercise because you think the team members don't respond well to that sort of discussion.

TEAMS - A Practical Guide

QUESTIONS

What are the key issues for the team?
_____
_____

What stage of team development do you think the team is currently in? Why?
_____
_____

What type of leadership style is the Manager using for the team?
Is this appropriate for the current stage of team development?
_____
_____

What's likely to happen when Emily joins the team?
What stage of team development will the team go to?
_____
_____

What could you do as the leader of the team to ensure that Emily integrates into the group?
_____
_____

As a member of the team, what could you do to move the team towards high performance?
_____
_____

As the leader of the team, and given the stage of team development,
what could you do to move the team towards high performance?
_____
_____

NOTES

CASE STUDY SUGGESTED ANSWER

Key Issues:

The key issue with the team is that it hasn't been deliberately led or managed. The team currently has open conflict, turnover and little direction or intervention from the Manager. It is also not operating effectively and achieving all its expected results, given there are issues with quality control.

The other issue is that the team is receiving a new member, someone who comes with a good reputation, is known to some members and is seen as high potential.

Current Stage of Team Development:

The team is most likely in the STORMING stage of team development. The team is characterised by conflict, division and sub-standard performance. The team is showing signs of asserting its independence by the recent challenging of the Leader's power and authority.

Current Leadership Style:

The Manager of the team seems to be using a delegated or 'hands-off' style of leadership. The Manager is giving little direction and appears to be avoiding the reality of the situation. This is precisely the wrong style of leadership that is required.

When Emily Joins the Team:

The team is likely to go briefly back to the Forming stage, with some politeness and veneer of team performance, however very quickly it will be further entrenched in the Storming stage. Given Emily is already known to some team members, new alliances and factions may be formed. Given she is a high potential employee, there may be some jealously and current team members may feel threatened. Teams in the Storming stage have the most trouble accepting new members as trust levels are low.

Integrating Emily into the Team

Emily needs to be formally introduced. Ideally a new member team session should be conducted, where expectations are outlined, roles are re-defined and interdependencies between team members explored. Emily also needs to be made aware of current team dynamics and issues. One on one meetings should be set up for Emily to personally meet each team member. Meetings should also be set up with key stakeholders and customers if appropriate. Emily should be inducted into team processes and ways of working through explanation and/or shadowing another team member. Emily could also be aligned with a buddy and external team mentor to help her integrate into the team.

Responsibility as a Team Member:

Given the team is in the Storming stage, with minimal trust and high dependence on the leader, the best course of action would be to go directly to the Leader of the team, either alone or with a preferred alliance. This conversation should be centred on current issues and suggestions for improvements. In the face of a delegative leadership style, team members need to take the initiative and influence the Leader to take more responsibility for the performance of the team by highlighting the consequences of what will happen if the status quo remains.

Responsibility as a Team Leader:

The team leader has high accountability at the Storming stage to develop the team. The leader needs to adopt a directive or coaching style of leadership as a priority. This would entail establishing clear communication around expectations and roles. It means providing proper resources and settings for the team members to do their work and form constructive relationships.

The Leader needs to hold a formal workshop where a team purpose and way of working are established and team principles are jointly agreed. The Leader needs to paint a vision of high performance and, together with the team, map the way to get there.

The Leader needs to confront the current conflict, get involved and seek resolution.

The Leader needs to check in regularly and at short intervals at the Storming stage and re-align expectations as necessary.

-end-

OTHER QUICK BITE TITLES

"Change: A Practical Guide for Dealing With and Managing Personal and Professional Change"
By Robin Elliott

E Book, PDF and Print Book
www.quickbites.co/products

Companion Product
Values Assessment Card Sort
www.quickbites.co/products

More titles coming on line soon.

WANT MORE INFORMATION?

Robin Elliott is available for keynote presentations, and business coaching.

If you found this book useful the good news is we have more titles coming on line.

Register your details at www.quickbites.co for updates.

QUICK BITES
BUSINESS LEARNING SOLUTIONS

www.ingramcontent.com/pod-product-compliance
Lightning Source LLC
Chambersburg PA
CBHW081126180526
45170CB00008B/3019